Stay Hopeful While You Study

ABOUT THE AUTHOR

Tania Richards Photography

Dr Dominique Thompson is a multi-award-winning GP, young people's mental health expert, TEDx speaker, author and educator, with two decades of clinical experience.

She is author of *The Student Wellbeing Series* (Trigger Publishing) for young people, and co-author of *How to Grow a Grown Up* (Penguin Random House) for parents. She has done two TEDx talks: "What I Learnt from 78,000 GP Consultations with University Students" and "Understanding Why".

Dom is a Clinical Advisor for NICE and Student Minds, and a Fellow of the Royal Society of Arts (FRSA). She is President-elect of the Student Health Association, and a member of the UK government's Higher Education Mental Health Implementation Taskforce. She was lead clinical advisor for Aardman Animation's *What's Up with Everyone?* campaign.

For further information about Dom's work, visit buzzconsulting.co.uk and check out growingagrownup.com for parenting support and free resources.

You can also follow her on Twitter and Instagram *@drdomthompson*.

Stay Hopeful While You Study

Make the Most of Your Student Experience

DR DOMINIQUE THOMPSON

This edition published in 2024 by Trigger Publishing
An imprint of Shaw Callaghan Ltd

UK Office
The Stanley Building
7 Pancras Square
Kings Cross
London N1C 4AG

US Office
On Point Executive Center, Inc
3030 N Rocky Point Drive W
Suite 150
Tampa, FL 33607
www.triggerpublishing.com

Text Copyright © 2019, 2024 Dominique Thompson
First published as *Depression at University* and *Depression at College*
by Trigger Publishing in 2019

Dominique Thompson has asserted her moral right to be identified as the author of this Work in accordance with the Copyright Designs and Patents Act 1988.

All rights reserved. No part of this publication may be reproduced, stored in a retrieval system, or transmitted in any form or by any means, electronically, mechanical, photocopying, recording or otherwise, without the prior permission of the copyright owners and the publishers.

A CIP catalogue record for this book is available upon request from the British Library
ISBN: 978-1-83796-304-1
eBook ISBN: 978-1-83796-305-8

Trigger Publishing encourages diversity and different viewpoints. However, all views, thoughts and opinions expressed in this book are the author's own and are not necessarily representative of us as an organization.

All material in this book is set out in good faith for general guidance and no liability can be accepted for loss or expense incurred in following the information given. In particular this book is not intended to replace expert medical or psychiatric advice. It is intended for informational purposes only and for your own personal use and guidance. It is not intended to act as a substitute for professional medical advice. Professional advice should be sought if desired before embarking on any health-related programme.

For Gareth. You're an inspiration – never give up.

ROLE DEFINITIONS

A who's who of student support

Doctor (general practitioner)
A medically qualified doctor who sees people in the community, not in a hospital, and is able to help with all conditions, although they may have a special interest, for example in skin problems or mental health. They are sometimes called a "family doctor", and will often refer patients to specialists, such as psychiatrists or psychologists, for specific problems.

Counselor
A counselor offers a safe, confidential space for individuals to talk. Counselors help their clients explore their thoughts, feelings and actions to help them come to terms with life and find more hopeful and useful ways to approach their future. Counselors will work in different ways, depending on their training, but will always allow their client to take the lead in what they want to talk about. They do not offer advice, but through the empathic attention they give to their client's words, the client often discovers their own wisdom, helping them to lead a more fulfilling life.

Clinical psychologist
A person who specializes in psychological or emotional conditions and mental health disorders. They will have specialized in the study of clinical psychology and usually

have a doctorate or PhD (though they're not medically qualified and will not be able to prescribe medication). They assess people and diagnose mental health conditions or problems. They are trained in using talking and behavioural interventions specifically tailored to treat psychological disorders. They may use a range of therapy approaches, including psychodynamic therapy, cognitive behavioural therapy, family and couples' therapies and interpersonal approaches. They base their assessment and treatment methods on scientific principles and outcomes and will use the best-evidenced method that helps to treat an individual.

Therapist

A term for professionals who use talking and behavioural therapies to support people with mental health conditions.

Psychiatrist

A medically qualified doctor who specializes in mental health conditions – also called psychiatric conditions – who can assess, make a diagnosis, offer advice and prescribe medication. A psychiatrist is the only person who can prescribe specialist medications. They work with other doctors, therapists, psychologists and counselors and will usually recommend a type of talking or behavioural treatment.

CONTENTS

Introduction 1

Chapter 1: What is Depression? 5

Chapter 2: How Do I Know if I Really Have Depression? ... 15

Chapter 3: More About Depression 21

Chapter 4: Types of Depression 25

Chapter 5: Are More People Experiencing Depression? 37

Chapter 6: Self-Harm and Suicidal Thoughts
and Feelings 41

Chapter 7: I Think I Have Depression –
What Do I Do Next? 49

Chapter 8: Helpful and Unhelpful Things People
Try to Alleviate Their Depression 59

Chapter 9: Behaviour Boosters 67

Chapter 10: Talking Therapies 75

Chapter 11: When Medication is the Next Step 79

Final Words 85

Additional Resources 89
References 91

INTRODUCTION

Depression can be exhausting and disabling, and it can take over your life. You no longer feel like "you" – and getting help can feel overwhelming. You've taken the first step by picking up this book! Well done. Keep going.

Having to support someone with depression is common and can be stressful and demanding, so this book will be helpful if you are worried about someone else.

Who should read this book?

If you feel any of the following symptoms, you might be struggling with depression. You may have several of these symptoms at once. They may not necessarily be related to depression, so talk to a professional if you:

- Feel numb, sad, down (depressed) or flat most of the time
- Regularly cry for no reason, or at things you don't feel you should cry about
- Feel inexplicably angry or irritable most of the time
- Think you are worthless or a failure
- Feel hopeless or helpless
- Feel tired all the time, even though you haven't done much to tire yourself
- Wake very early every day or feel unrefreshed from sleep in the mornings
- Have started having "brain fog"

- Can't concentrate on your work or study, or your focus is really poor
- Find it hard to make daily decisions, such as what to eat, what to wear, what to watch or do, and so on
- Have stopped caring for yourself or your appearance
- Have stopped doing things you used to enjoy
- Can't be bothered to do things if they're too much effort or your motivation is poor
- No longer enjoy life or the activities that you used to enjoy
- Have isolated yourself from people you used to spend time with because you don't want to be a "burden"
- Find that your appetite has gone or that you eat too much ("comforting eating")
- Have lost interest in sex
- Harm yourself to relieve your emotional pain or distract yourself from it
- Think about dying or believe that there's no point in being alive
- Think about ending your life, or believe that others would be "better off" without you
- Feel guilty for being alive or that you don't deserve to be happy
- Feel trapped or can't see how life might get better
- Don't necessarily want to die, but don't want to be alive either

Why should you read this book?

Reading this book will help you to:

- Learn more about what depression is and about the different types of depression
- Tackle some of the myths around depression
- Know more about self-harm and suicidal thoughts
- Learn about some of the causes of these feelings
- Consider whether you might have depression

- Know when and where to get help and who to speak to about it
- Better understand what help might be offered, and what might help you
- Understand which therapies are recommended for different types of depression
- Know what to try for yourself that might help, and what might make it worse
- Get a sense of which medications are available and what you might be offered, if appropriate
- Know where to get further help and consider next steps

This book will tell you what you need to know if you have depression and / or if you self-harm or have suicidal thoughts because you are depressed.

> **Important point**
> If you are struggling with your wellbeing, it is vital to let your university know what is happening with you. That way, they can make sure that you receive the right support and ensure fairness in any assessment they make of you and your work.
>
> Every university will have a process for what are called "mitigating" or "extenuating" circumstances (special circumstances that may have an impact on your academic performance, including physical and mental health issues, bereavement, and other significant life events). These can happen to anyone, so make sure that you let the university know. Talk to your tutor, complete the necessary forms, and get the support you need and deserve.

CHAPTER 1

WHAT IS DEPRESSION?

Depression is not just "feeling sad". It is an illness that can affect your mood, thoughts and behaviours.

In a student's own words

A student who was a patient of mine wrote this to explain how he felt when he was depressed. It explains, eloquently and movingly, how depression affected him (Student Health Doc Blogs, 2013). Gareth is now recovered and works as a university lecturer; he speaks out about mental health issues in young people.

> *I'm sick of waking up every morning and just being unbelievably tired. I never get to not feel tired, especially now. And it's so frustrating because when I'm not tired, or when I'm working well, then I'm actually pretty good. But when I'm not I'm just awful; I can't work and it's horrible. I literally have, very briefly, seen how good I can be, and that's always in my head somewhere being chased around and held down by being suicidal, and being always tired, and full of self-hatred and guilt and regret. I don't know how to get it out, or bring it to the forefront.*

> *I think suicide is different now: it's not actively wanting to die, it's wanting to not exist, because existence is 90% tiredness and guilt and regret and hate, and trying and failing to cover all of that up.* – **Gareth**

This is such an emotional and descriptive expression of Gareth's depression, the exhaustion of just living through each day, and his negative thoughts about himself. It is important to say that depression does not always make you feel suicidal, but it can certainly lead to thoughts of suicide for some people. We will talk about that more later.

I hope that reading Gareth's description will help you to understand that you are not alone if you feel similar to this, or perhaps it might help you to better support a friend who you think is depressed.

What does depression feel like?
You feel sad or empty
For many people, depression makes them feel empty, numb, nothing, or just sad, but not always about anything in particular. You might feel that there is no point in doing anything, like getting up out of bed or leaving your room or the house. You might feel there is no point in eating, washing, or dressing. You may believe that no one else cares about how you are feeling, or that you are not worth caring about. You might feel like a burden, that you are "in the way" of other people having a good time or living their lives, and that you're just an obstacle for them to have to deal with or manage. In short, you feel negative (or nothing) about almost everything.

You are angry or irritable

Depression can also make you feel angry and / or *really* irritable, with both strangers and the people you love. You might get angry at other shoppers in the supermarket, passengers on the bus, noisy kids in your street, or your family and friends or housemates. Nothing they do is right – it all just gets on your nerves and can make you feel desperate or behave in an aggressive way. They may notice or comment that you are "snappy" or "moody", when in fact you are depressed.

You are indecisive

Depression can make you unable to make simple decisions. You might stand for ages in the local store trying to decide which sandwich to buy, unable to choose and not really caring. You might not be able to decide what to watch on TV, or you could find that your attention span is affected; maybe you just scroll through a streaming platform or flick between different websites on your laptop. If you are asked what you want to eat you don't care; if your friends ask if you want to go out with them you just can't decide what to do.

You are tearful

Depression can make you tearful and you might find yourself crying most days – at your desk, in the library, playing sports, or sitting with friends. Sometimes it can be because of something sad on the news or a cute video, but often your tears and sorrow are for no reason. It's nothing you can explain, but sometimes a feeling of deep sadness may overwhelm you.

Your sleep is disrupted

Depression can affect your sleep patterns. You may want to sleep all the time, curled up under a duvet, hiding from the world, exhausted from doing nothing and feeling down. You may feel shattered and desperate for rest but unable to sleep. Your mind might be whirring, or you might feel agitated. Sometimes depression makes you restless and unable to drop off to sleep, even if you're bone tired. Sometimes it wakes you early, often at about 4am – it's even got a name, Early Morning Wakening, because it's such a well-recognized symptom. Sleeping in the day feels like the only way to cope, but this can make sleeping at night even more difficult, and a vicious cycle begins. You might find yourself sleeping too much – maybe for hours and hours, maybe half the day as well as the night, and yet still feel tired (or unrefreshed) when you wake up. It's exhausting.

You might use cigarettes, alcohol and / or drugs

Some people try to manage their sleep issues, irritability and restlessness by smoking, drinking and using a variety of non-prescribed drugs to cope. But while these may feel like a short-term fix, they will usually make a challenging situation much worse in the longer term. We will come back to this later.

Your eating patterns are disrupted

Depression can affect your appetite. You may find yourself wanting to eat a lot of fast food or "comfort" foods such as toast, chocolate, cakes and snacks so that you don't have to make much effort. The eating itself can be an act of self-care; giving yourself treats to lift your mood. Sometimes you will feel better for a short while after eating such foods, but with time such a diet will make you feel stodgy, lethargic and unhealthy, which could possibly make the depression worse.

Depression can, of course, make you lose your appetite. Indecisiveness about activities can also include eating, so sometimes making decisions about food can feel too difficult. You might avoid eating completely or just survive on foods like toast or cereal – things that involve little effort but give a quick energy boost. Weight loss can follow swiftly.

Appetite changes are one of the reasons that those with depression often notice weight changes (both up and down) when they are low.

You are tired all the time and have lost your motivation

Feeling "tired all the time" is so common among patients that doctors even have an acronym for it: TATT. It's a very real problem for people who are depressed. It can feel as if all the energy has drained out of you. Lethargy overwhelms you and you lose motivation or enthusiasm for many of the things that you have previously enjoyed doing, such as meeting up with friends, sports, reading, sewing or walking the dog. Everything is too much effort. You stop going to university clubs or societies, and hide in your room or slump in front of the TV. Turning up for your Saturday job almost kills you, and going out with mates in the evenings is a no-go. Sex is of no interest. You make excuses to avoid going out, telling people you're "shattered" and having a quiet one, but in fact you just can't drag yourself out. If it gets worse, then even washing and looking after basic hygiene can become a problem for some depressed students.

You feel like you have "brain fog"

For many students, one of the reasons that they finally seek professional support and help is because of the effect depression has on their academic work. They can no longer concentrate, focus or study. They can't understand the texts they are reading and may have to read the same phrase or paragraph several times for it to stick. They find their memory is poor (made worse by their disrupted sleep) and they struggle to keep up with academic deadlines. Having been hard workers or high achievers and never really having "failed" at anything in the past, this particular aspect of depression can be a terrible blow for them. It may lead some to feel particularly down, think that they are failures, or even in some cases to think about suicide. The *depression* prevents them from seeing the world clearly and understanding that this is not "them" – this is the illness. It is affecting their brain and cognitive (thinking) processes.

You feel worthless, guilty and ashamed

Being depressed can make dealing with other people a particular stress. Coping with other people's moods, expectations and demands can be tiring at the best of times, so when you are feeling down it can be extremely challenging. Staying polite and patient, and even just replying in a civil manner can take it out of you. Some people might place expectations on you, such as to work hard or live up to past academic achievements. They may be supporting you in both financial and emotional ways, and you might feel that you can't – or don't want to – let them down. This is really tough. You have an illness called depression, but for lots of reasons it can be hard to admit this to people. You might not have realized yourself that you are suffering from it yet, so it can be tough to explain why you aren't feeling up to chatting or why you are struggling to keep up with your work and what you believe are their expectations. This can then make you feel more depressed and sometimes even worthless, guilty or ashamed.

You feel agitated and restless

As we have said, many people who are depressed feel slowed down or lethargic, but there are some who actually become more restless. They might pace, twitch, pick at their skin and / or feel agitated. This is usually more likely in those who have the "angry" kind of depression, rather than the "sad" kind. It is also seen in bipolar depression, which we will describe later on.

You may notice yourself becoming increasingly irritated, aggressive or uncooperative. In some cases, you may become hostile or violent, though this is not always the case. It can feel like a build-up of pressure which you may try to get rid of by moving around or pacing. It feels very uncomfortable and should not be ignored.

You have poor self-esteem and low self-confidence

As you start to feel down and the depression sets in, it may be that you turn some of that negative feeling on yourself. You may start to doubt or criticize yourself more. You might be harsh on yourself for not achieving the things you think you should be achieving, and this can then make you feel more down and possibly a "failure". You can get stuck on thoughts about yourself such as, *"I'm so hopeless and I can't even do this,"* comparing yourself negatively to others around you. These first negative thoughts can lead to others such as, *"No wonder people don't want to be my friend if I'm this useless,"* or, *"I don't deserve to be happy / have friends / succeed."*

The vicious spiral of negative thoughts can be very hard to escape, and of course it continues to undermine your confidence in yourself and your ability to do things that you are perfectly able to do – and that you may have done well before, in fact. Depression can make you feel terrible about yourself, and even, in some cases, can cause you to hate yourself. Worst of all, it stops you living the life you should be leading, causing you to hide away from the world, avoiding people and activities you used to enjoy, and falsely making you believe that you are not a worthwhile and lovely person.

You are self-harming

Sometimes, when you feel bleak, the emotional pain can be so overwhelming that it leads you to physically harm yourself. The new physical pain may then distract you from the internal emotional pain for a while and give you something different to think about. This is how some people who self-harm describe the reasoning behind them harming themselves. Others describe their feelings as a "boiling pot with a lid on which is threatening to blow", and the self-harm is the equivalent of taking the lid off the boiling pot, releasing the pressure inside and allowing them to feel almost calm again.

The act of cutting, burning and other ways of self-harming can give you a great sense of relief, but it is important to recognize that it is still a symptom of underlying distress. It can also be a high-risk activity as accidental fatalities can happen. Scarring, bleeding and infection are all potentially serious consequences. Trying to deal with the emotional pain that leads to self-harm can be a positive step in the right direction for long-term wellbeing and health, although it can be difficult to deal with.

You have suicidal thoughts and feelings

It may surprise you to know that suicidal thoughts and feelings are common – about 1 in 5 people will think about suicide at some point in their lives (Lee et al., 2010). This topic will be covered in much more detail in Chapter 6 to ensure that these thoughts and feelings get the time and recognition that they deserve. Suicidal thoughts can be scary or strangely comforting, but the key thing here is to recognize them as a *symptom* of depression and not to ignore them, and to talk to someone about how you are feeling.

Physical symptoms of depression

We have talked a lot so far about the emotions or feelings you can get with depression, and these are generally well recognized, even if it can take time to accept that you may need help. But it is less well known that you can suffer from physical symptoms with depression too.

The brain processes that cause us to feel sad, tearful or angry can also upset other bodily functions, such as pain and immune system pathways.

Pain can get worse

It is therefore quite common for you to feel pain differently if you have depression, and those with chronic pain conditions can suffer particularly badly. Back and neck pain, headaches and migraines can all get worse, as can digestive or tummy upsets and dizzy spells. We have already talked about sleep and appetite, and when these are derailed by depression, then physical health and energy levels will naturally go downhill too.

Immune system is weaker or "misfires"

There has been a lot of research over the last few decades looking at how depression and the immune system interact, and it seems that while people who had been treated for a severe infection were 62% more likely to have developed a mood disorder than those who never had one (Benros et al., 2013), it is also possible that depression itself is an immune response, with stress (from life events, for example) causing immune changes in your brain, which can lead to depression (Nie et al., 2018).

All of these emotions, feelings, behaviours and physiological changes can be symptoms of depression, so let's consider when and how you might be able to ask for help.

CHAPTER 2

HOW DO I KNOW IF I REALLY HAVE DEPRESSION?

One thing that university doctors learn through experience is that everyone is different in how they describe depression, but there are also some things that many people have in common. Most students go to see the doctor when they can't think straight anymore, when their concentration, focus and motivation are almost gone, and when they feel consistently flat, empty or numb.

If reading through the lists and descriptions in this book makes you feel as though you are ticking off a checklist and saying "Yes, yes, yes" to many of the symptoms, then you should take the next step, and talk to a trusted family member or friend – and then a professional – about how you are feeling. Help is available.

Ask yourself this

It is important to recognize that we all feel some of the feelings and emotions covered in Chapter 1 sometimes, so the question to ask yourself about these feelings is this:

Am I feeling these things most or all of the time, most days and for more than about two weeks? (In other words, are these difficult feelings pervasive and persistent?)

So, for example, if you have been feeling down, irritable, unable to sleep properly and exhausted on most days for more than two weeks, then you should seek help and advice from a professional and support from a friend or family member. You may well have depression.

Similarly, if you have been crying most days for more than two weeks, or thinking that your friends and loved ones would be "better off" if you weren't around, then you should also seek support and advice without delay. This may also be depression, rather than just a "bad patch". Discussion with a professional will make clear what is happening for you.

Hiding the symptoms of depression

Some people may feel low, sad or irritable, but can manage to hide their feelings from those around them. They "put on a brave face" or mask how they are feeling, and they act in an apparently "normal" way day to day, but inside they are struggling and may feel quite desperate.

If you recognize yourself in this – if you are someone who tries to keep going despite feeling dreadful – then you are not alone. But it is still a really good idea to go and talk to someone about it. It is common for students to be reluctant to show how they are feeling, as they may be worried about being asked to leave the university or prevented from studying their chosen course. But, in fact, if you seek help then the university should support you and offer services such as advice, therapy or medical care.

Vocational students

Particular groups of students on vocational courses such as medicine, dentistry or veterinary sciences may be even more worried about declaring a mental health issue. They might try to push through their depression and suicidal thoughts because of their worries around "Fitness to Practise" and other similar policies.

It is really important to remember that in order to be a good, effective healthcare professional you need to look after *yourself* first, and that all the professional organizations, such as the General Medical Council and so on, are very clear that they actively support and encourage their colleagues to get help and show insight into their own needs for emotional support (General Medical Council, 2015).

In other words, if you are depressed as a student, the university should support you, and if you are depressed as a vocational course student, your professional standards organization should respect and support you in getting help too – and so it will be seen as a positive thing for you to do.

Depression and other conditions

It is really common for people with depression to also have other problems to manage. Some of these may be mental health issues such as anxiety, and some may be long-term physical conditions such as diabetes. Let's think about what this might mean for you if you think this might be your situation.

Depression with anxiety

If you are diagnosed with depression, you have a 1 in 2 chance of being diagnosed with anxiety too (World Health Organization, 2018). In other words, about half of students who have depression have anxiety as well. So, if you aren't just feeling down or flat but you're also worried all the time, on edge and nervous, then you may well have anxiety alongside your depression.

They will both need treatment, but the good news is that there are effective ways to manage both conditions together.

This is also the case for depression with other *anxiety-related* disorders such as social anxiety, phobias and obsessive-compulsive disorder. Don't ignore one of these conditions to focus on the other, or be misled into thinking you can't have both, because unfortunately you can. And it's common.

Depression with other mental health conditions

Students with eating disorders, schizophrenia, substance misuse conditions and Attention Deficit Hyperactivity Disorder (ADHD) are also more likely to suffer from depression. It may be that having these conditions makes life harder in various ways and that is what leads people to feel depressed, or it may be that the depression is unrelated to the other mental health disorder and related instead to life events or genetic tendency.

If you believe you are one of these students, you will certainly need treatment and advice about managing your conditions in order to achieve your potential and navigate your academic and career pathways.

Depression with physical health conditions

Doctors need to bear in mind that any student coming to visit them with depressive symptoms might have an underlying *physical* condition, such as a thyroid hormone imbalance, diabetes, or Chronic Fatigue Syndrome. This fact does sometimes get overlooked in the day-to-day pressure of doctors' appointments, unfortunately.

Essentially, the thyroid gland sits in the front of the neck and produces hormones that are crucial for a healthy metabolism, including processes for weight management, energy levels, bowel function, and hair and skin changes, to name a few. So, when the thyroid gland stops working properly, it can *mimic* symptoms of depression and affect your mood directly. Thyroid disorders and depression often get mistaken for each other, but a simple blood test will clarify the cause of the symptoms.

Depression is also more common in other conditions such as diabetes and heart disease (Mental Health America, 2018) and is sometimes caused by particular medications, for example some acne medications, or certain brands of the contraceptive pill.

This is why it is important that if you are seeing a doctor for your mood, then you should also be prepared to answer sensitive questions about your physical symptoms, any medicines that you may be taking and your family history of mental health issues.

CHAPTER 3

MORE ABOUT DEPRESSION

Causes of depression

For those of you who would like to know a bit more about what might be *causing* your depression, this chapter will outline some of the current theories that are being investigated by scientists around the world. Other theories exist which describe behavioural causes, or the combination of biological, psychological and social factors, known as the biopsychosocial theory of depression.

Does depression run in families?

There is clear evidence that depression is about 50% inherited and 50% environment effect (Levinson and Nichols, 2023), but it is unlikely to be a simple process. It is probable that you might have inherited a genetic tendency, and then certain factors in your environment as you grow up and develop affect whether or not you develop depression – and if so, how bad it may be.

So, if your mum or dad had depression, it is more likely that you will also develop it, but this will partly depend on other influences from your surroundings and lifestyle.

Groups of people who are more prone to depression

Unfortunately, some people are more likely to develop depression than others. Women are more at risk than men, for example, as are people with long-term conditions like cancer and diabetes. Adults aged 18 to 29 years old are more likely to suffer than any other age group. When race is considered, African Americans are more at risk than their Caucasian peers in the US, as are Black and Black British people in the UK (Mind). When minorities are disproportionately affected by health conditions, sadly we see an inequality of access to support, treatment and assessment for healthcare, leading to significantly poorer outcomes and mental health (Bignall et al., 2019).

Neuroplasticity theory of depression

This theory puts forward the idea that the brain develops according to influences from external stresses (Liu et al., 2017). Negative influences might include bereavement, loss and emotional trauma in childhood.

It can help to imagine your brain like a bonsai tree. Normally the tree grows and the pruning that occurs to shape it would represent the normal "pruning" of nerve pathways. The theory states that negative stresses can then influence the pruning, causing the brain (tree) to grow in unusual or abnormal ways, creating new nerve pathways (branches), in particular allowing the area responsible for anxiety and fear (called the *amygdala*) to steadily grow larger.

Thus, your future reactions are disproportionately more negative as you grow older if you have a lot of negative influences on your brain development.

Some evidence shows that therapy and medication can re-set the nerve growth, but that will obviously take time, hence the need to keep going with any treatments that you start.

Immune theory of depression

This is the theory of how the immune system might affect your mood.

The guilty party in this theory is essentially a group of brain (neuro) transmitters (chemicals) called "cytokines", which *reduce* the making of serotonin and dopamine, two of the "happy hormones" in the brain (Raison, Capuron and Miller, 2006).

Cytokines also *increase* how much cortisol (steroid) hormone your brain produces and, as this is your "stress response" hormone used for regulating your blood pressure, blood sugars and metabolism, your body will respond as if it is under stress. This affects sleep, appetite, weight and your "fight or flight" reactions (Rakesh, 2018). This may be partly why so many people with long-term conditions, like diabetes and arthritis, also suffer from depression.

CHAPTER 4

TYPES OF DEPRESSION

Depression (mild, moderate and severe)

Depression is not about feeling "a bit sad or low" for a few days. It is a real illness and causes people to feel down, flat, empty or numb, day in, day out, for weeks, months or even years at a time.

However, it is important to say that many people *continue to function* and go through the motions of life, work and responsibilities, even when they are suffering from depression (usually mild to moderate), but they are likely to feel uninterested and unmotivated, lack enthusiasm and, frankly, be irritable as they do so.

Not everyone with depression reaches the point of retreating to their bed or sofa and being unable to do the things they want to do – though when that does happen, it can be devastating.

Depression is generally described as being mild, moderate or severe according to the range of symptoms, their persistence and pervasiveness and how badly you are affected by them.

Treatment approaches for the three categories tend to be different, with mild depression generally needing mainly talking therapy for successful improvement, and moderate-to-severe symptoms usually requiring both medication and talking therapies. If symptoms are very severe, the sufferer may need medication to get them to a point where they can actually take part in talking therapy, because if you are severely depressed you may not be able to engage usefully in conversation and critical thought about your mood and what helpful steps to take next.

There are good screening questionnaires for depression, so when you go and talk to a counselor, psychologist or doctor about your symptoms, it is likely that they will ask you to complete a brief series of questions about your mood, sleep, appetite and thoughts of self-harm or suicide. This will help them to diagnose and classify your depression, and share with you a plan for treatment.

> **Sofia's story – mild depression**
> Sofia was halfway through her final year of studies and feeling under pressure. She was feeling pretty anxious too. She had noticed herself becoming irritable with her boyfriend and housemates and then feeling guilty. She had stopped going out quite as much, wasn't really as interested in sex anymore, and she was crying out of the blue at sad news or TV programmes. However, on other days, she was able to get on with her work, join in her normal activities such as playing squash and sit around chatting with her friends. She couldn't quite work out what was wrong – was she being grumpy, or was there more to it?
>
> She went to speak with an advisor, and they talked about it. She completed a questionnaire, and they chatted through the results. It seemed Sofia had mild depression – not bad enough to need a doctor's appointment or

medication, but definitely at a level where counseling or a talking therapy such as CBT might be helpful. A few weeks later – after having been for weekly sessions at the student counseling service, increasing exercise, improving sleep patterns and reducing alcohol intake – Sofia was feeling back to normal, on top of her academic work and able to do all the activities she wanted to in the run-up to her final exams. She was glad she hadn't left it any longer before getting help, as otherwise she might have been more seriously unwell, and treatment would have taken longer, during a critical point in her studies.

Bo's story – moderate depression

Bo was an international student and had been at the university for several months. He came to the doctor because he had lost a bit of weight and was not sleeping well. He was concerned he might have a physical illness, giving him what he described as a "brain fog", causing him to feel tired most of the time and resulting in him feeling less hungry. He couldn't think clearly and his work was suffering.

He was under a lot of pressure from home to do well at university, but was struggling to acclimatize to some aspects of his surroundings such as the weather, food and language. He told the doctor that most days he felt "not himself" and there wasn't much let up in his negative feelings. He was either tired or irritable, and some weeks he just felt flat. He could still go to lectures, meet up with friends and so on, but he was not enjoying things anymore. He had briefly thought that life might not be worth living, but was not suicidal, although the thoughts had frightened him.

The doctor took time to explore the physical symptoms – depression can lead to weight loss as well as other conditions such as thyroid disorders. They also discussed blood tests. They talked about possible emotional or psychological causes of his distress and planned to meet again when Bo had had time to think about such causes and his options for helping himself to get better though exercise, better sleep habits, good dietary choices and minimal alcohol, as well as possible medication and therapy.

Over the next weeks and months they met regularly. Bo started seeing a psychologist for CBT and he slowly recovered from his depressive episode. His studies continued and he took more care to look after himself, as he realized how important this was to avoid a future similar situation.

Anika's story – severe depression

Anika came into the doctor's consulting room slowly. She looked dishevelled, exhausted and thin, and did not meet the doctor's eye. Sitting on the chair, she stared at the floor and spoke slowly, answering the doctor's questions in a flat voice. She said she had come as a "last resort". She was feeling "numb" and wondered if there was anything the doctor could do to help. She had lost interest in everything. She had stopped getting out of bed most days and was not washing. She couldn't remember when she last ate, but it was probably a day or two ago. She thought about suicide a lot and had cuts to her abdomen and thighs where she had harmed herself to relieve her emotional pain. Anika looked at the doctor with sad eyes and a hopeless expression.

They started to talk and make a plan. It was Anika's choice, but medication such as antidepressants would likely be of benefit in a case of severe depression such as this. Then they would meet every week initially to check on progress and review the medication.

As Anika improved, she could start a therapy such as CBT. There were other support options available, such as online resources and peer-to-peer groups, and her friends were keen to help. Over the next few months Anika slowly improved, her mood lifted and returned to normal, and she was supported by her academic department to catch up with her work. Anika made a good recovery over time, and was able to fully engage with her studies and friends with the right kind of help.

Seasonal affective disorder (SAD)

This is a mood change which can come over you as the seasons change (NHS, 2022). As the days become darker for longer, the weather gets colder, and the winter sets in, it is not uncommon to notice a flatness of mood, an urge to stay in and "hibernate", a need to sleep a lot more and eat more carbs. Weight gain can follow and feelings of guilt and hopelessness may come over you. Then, as the springtime arrives, the sun returns, and the days get longer. Your mood lifts and suddenly all feels well again with the world.

It can take years for people to recognize this pattern of depression in winter. It may be worth thinking back over the times you have felt low in your life and see if you spot a *seasonal* pattern.

> **Matt's story**
>
> Matt was a second-year postgraduate student, struggling with his workload. He came to see the student support team unsure of what help he needed. "I think I'm turning into a hamster," he said, still managing to smile weakly. "I ave so much work to do, but all I want to do is sleep, stay in bed and eat junk food. And I have no interest in doing anything anymore." The student advisor listened and asked if Matt had felt like this before. It turned out that he had.
>
> Every time the clock went back in the autumn and the days got shorter, all Matt wanted to do was hide away. He felt low and unmotivated, and it was proving disastrous for his academic work. They talked for a while; the advisor mentioned the possibility of SAD and some of the things that Matt might like to read about and try, such as more exercise, getting natural daylight each day, a lightbox (SAD light) on his desk in the mornings, perhaps CBT or even medication from a doctor if things were too difficult or not improving.
>
> Matt was intrigued to realize that his symptoms had a name and that the seasonal pattern was key. He left the meeting feeling relieved and keen to try some of the suggested measures.

Bipolar disorder

This book is mainly focused on depression, but it would be wrong not to mention a closely related condition called bipolar disorder (formerly known as manic depression).

People with this condition tend to have extremes of mood. A pattern develops, moving from depression and despair through to feelings of being very "high", "up" or overactive and extremely happy. Some sufferers may only rarely feel "normal".

Some people with bipolar disorder may experience psychosis; they might hear voices or see things that aren't actually there but which feel very real. They can be convinced of quite unusual beliefs when they are "manic", such as that they are a messiah or that they have great talents, for example exceptional musical ability or the ability to fly. At a less-extreme level, before people become "manic" they may be considered "hypomanic".

In a manic phase, those with bipolar disorder may stop sleeping for days on end, feel very creative, see the world in brighter colours and feel extremely energized. They can be reckless in many ways, even, unfortunately, allowing themselves to be vulnerable to danger. They may have a heightened sex drive and seek out sex with strangers, spend money they don't have, or phone friends in the middle of the night with "amazing" ideas, but actually make little sense to others. They might talk at great speed as their ideas race around their minds.

Am I bipolar?

It is common for students ask the question "Am I bipolar?" Many young people worry that they have bipolar disorder because they experience mood swings. It is therefore helpful and important to differentiate between normal mood ups and downs, which can occur within the space of a day or a few days, and the persistent lows and then highs of bipolar disorder, which can each last for days or weeks.

When untreated, bipolar disorder can make it impossible to function normally, to work and study, or have relationships. Sleep can be extremely difficult, and you may stop eating. These more serious symptoms are unlikely to be present if you are having normal mood swings or even mild depression.

Those with mild depression can often worry it is actually bipolar if they have noticed that their mood is low, but then they have a good day or two when they feel productive and happy. As the depression at this stage is mild, it is not persistent every day, so it can be perceived as being interrupted by "up" phases which are actually just a normal mood. It is understandable that these young people then wonder if they have bipolar disorder, but talking this through with a doctor or psychologist will clarify the symptoms and patterns of mood, and should reassure the vast majority that this is not likely to be bipolar.

Most people experiencing a manic phase (or early mania, such as hypomania) don't actually realize they are unwell until other people notice and advise that they need help. If in doubt, the following advice from Bipolar UK may be helpful (there are also formal screening questionnaires which professionals may use to assess you): keep a mood diary / mood scale for a few weeks to monitor fluctuations and clarify whether there are extremes of high or low / suicidal mood. Take this with you to an appointment with a professional (2018).

Julia's story

Julia was a dental student, a high achiever with lots of friends and a very busy life at university. Her friends brought her to the counseling service one day as they were worried about her behaviour. They explained that she was staying up for several nights at a time, writing what she said was music, but which made no sense to anyone else. They were also worried because she had been bringing various young men back to their flat and having a lot of sex, which was out of character for her. She seemed to be behaving very excitedly all the time.

Julia agreed that these things were happening, but brushed them off because she felt "brilliant" and was keen to share her thoughts about how her musical ability might lead the world to "be a better place". Over the course of the conversation, it became clear that Julia had been depressed in the past, but that she had been feeling "up" for almost two weeks. She was not at all concerned about this.

It was agreed that she needed a medical assessment, and in time she was reviewed by a psychiatrist. She was diagnosed with bipolar disorder and a treatment plan was agreed. Her friends continued to support her, and her mum came to stay for a while as Julia started medication and talking therapy. She had a break from her studies and the university was very supportive as she recovered from her manic phase. In time she returned to her studies and was able to qualify as a dentist, while managing her bipolar disorder successfully and with support.

Grief, loss and bereavement

It is normal when suffering from grief, loss or bereavement to feel very (sometimes extremely) sad, to lose your appetite (and maybe a bit of weight) and be unable to sleep properly. We are only human, and humans have always mourned certain life events, such as the loss of a loved one, separation from our nearest and dearest, leaving home, or moving abroad. It may, as a process, actually help us to move on and heal from things too. Depression and grief can exist together, but it is important to allow a few weeks or even months after a difficult event has occurred before assuming that you should be feeling normal and well and functioning as you were before.

Sometimes students seek medical advice *the day after* a long-term relationship has ended because "I'm still crying, and I haven't got time to be sad". They have been unrealistic about how long a person needs to recover from loss and deal with grief. Clearly, in such situations we need to be kind to ourselves, allow ourselves to grieve properly for the loss of the relationship and our future dreams, and process such traumatic situations. We need to move on gradually.

One of the main ways to *differentiate grief from depression* is to look at whether the sadness, tears and exhaustion gradually fade and are balanced by happy memories and an ability to rationalize the events with time, or whether the anger, guilt and negativity is internalized, making you feel hopeless, worthless, and possibly even suicidal as time goes on.

Jake's story

Jake was a first-year student who had arrived at university after a gap year. He told the therapist the story of that year: how he and his girlfriend had gone travelling after leaving school, and how, in a terrible bus crash, she had been killed a few weeks before he came to university. He was also injured, but after several weeks of treatment he had recovered well enough to begin school as planned.

With the focus of the last few weeks being on his recovery and then packing for university, he now wanted to talk about his grief at the loss of his best friend and partner. He wanted to make time to process with his emotions at a challenging time of transition. He and the therapist were able to meet regularly as he settled into university life, dealing with his guilt at having survived the crash. He wanted to remember his girlfriend and make her proud of him while looking to his future emotional needs.

Jake did not become depressed, but he did have times of sadness, loneliness and introspection when he would think about what might have been. He was also, with help, able to look forward and manage his difficult emotions, allowing himself to thrive at university as the years went on.

CHAPTER 5

ARE MORE PEOPLE EXPERIENCING DEPRESSION?

There has been a steady increase in the number of young people developing depression, according to studies in both the UK and the USA. In the UK 2 in 5 (40%) 16-to-25-year-olds have experienced depression or feeling down at some time in their lives (Statista, 2021). Ten years prior it was 30%. In the US more than one third of women and 1 in 5 men will be diagnosed with depression at some point in their lives (Gallup, 2023).

Why is depression increasing?

It seems fair to say that young people are under pressure like no previous generation. A whole variety of factors are combining to create what can feel like a "pressure cooker society", and it is therefore no surprise that more young people seem to be developing mental health conditions, with depression being one of the commonest. Rates of depression were rising before the pandemic but the impact of COVID-19 on young adult mental health has been significantly negative, leading to even higher numbers suffering from depression than previously expected.

Competitiveness

We have become a society where even the fun stuff has become a competition. Baking cakes, photography, painting, singing and dancing; we now think of these as a type of "competitive sport". Whether it's done by kids at school or celebrities on TV, we are surrounded, worldwide, by relentless competition.

And this is particularly true in the university or college lecture hall and tutorial room, where students no longer feel pressure to simply "get a broad education" or even just a degree, but to get a top-class qualification, then a postgrad degree or other diploma, in a never-ending race to the top. This pressure risks exhausting a whole generation.

Perfectionism

Closely linked to the overly competitive nature of our society is the documented rise in perfectionism among young adults (Curran and Hill, 2017). Perfectionism is striving for impossibly high standards and refusing to accept anything less than perfection. You can be highly self-critical and feel that any mistake is unacceptable. The level of universal competitiveness seems to have driven a huge increase in the number of students with perfectionist traits in the US, Canada and the UK over the last 30 or so years. With perfectionist traits being closely linked to several mental health conditions, such as anxiety, depression, self-harm, eating disorders and obsessive-compulsive disorders, it starts to become apparent why doctors and counselors may be seeing more students with these conditions, through no fault of their own.

Trying to keep up with everyone else, trying to be *the* best – not just doing *your* best – might in some cases make you ill.

Social media

So now let's magnify all of that competition and perfectionism with social media.

The lens of Instagram for example can really pile on the pressure. Not only are students driving themselves harder than ever before, but they are being "monitored" and "graded" 24/7 via their own social media channels. Social media in itself may not be causing depression in many cases, but it may be making a difficult situation worse. For some of you, social media *will* be the source of depression (e.g., seeing traumatic events online), or it might fuel obsessive tendencies and the seeking of reassurance, driving the need for "likes" or followers, or by playing into body image insecurities, making you feel worse. For some students with eating or food issues, social media can be a source of damaging and even dangerous information about weight loss or cosmetic and surgical interventions. The pressure to alter your appearance can depress your mood and make it harder to seek help.

It's important to remember, though, that for a lot of people social media can also be a source of support and useful resources, particularly if they suffer from mental health problems that leave them feeling isolated and disconnected – it can offer a way of connecting with other people.

Other stresses – for example, money

There are other significant stresses for you, of course, with academic pressure the number one cause of student distress and suicide, sadly (University of Manchester, 2018). This is closely followed by money worries, family issues, health problems and relationship difficulties. Other stresses might include bullying, housing issues and workplace issues. Online bullying and harassment in particular have risen in recent years, with some students having to manage difficult scenarios involving ex-partners or strangers stalking them. The university can often help in such situations, offering advice and support, for example through Independent Sexual Violence Advisors if sexual assault has occurred.

Family and friends, who should be a source of support, can often be a cause of distress, for example through arguments with housemates, parental conflict or divorce, parental alcohol use, or friends' own mental health issues.

Loneliness and isolation

Loneliness and isolation have been an issue for some students for many years, but the pandemic made this a challenge for lots of students in a way that it hadn't been in the past. Disconnection from friends and family and the impact of lockdown is one of the biggest causes of mental health issues – in particular, depression – for young adults post-pandemic (Owens et al., 2022).

Many students are taking to the internet to write blogs about their lonely life, so if you often feel isolated, then you are not the only student feeling like this. Obviously, if you are feeling depressed, that may make it harder for you to meet people, and then if you become isolated it can make your mood worse. So, this can be a bit of a vicious cycle.

All these different pressures can really build up at a time of transition and academic expectation. It is therefore unsurprising that depression is on the rise. We will look at ways to tackle these issues later in this book.

CHAPTER 6

SELF-HARM AND SUICIDAL THOUGHTS AND FEELINGS

> Warning: This chapter contains information that may be distressing to read and consider. Please talk to someone you trust if you feel upset by it.

Self-harm

Imagine a bubbling pot on a high heat on the stove in front of you. It's under pressure because it has a lid on it. Then imagine you take that lid off the pot. That sense of relief that comes from letting out the pressure and steam is how many people who self-harm describe the relief they feel from causing themselves physical pain and injury. They experience so much emotional pressure that hurting themselves physically allows some of that pressure to be released and a sense of calm to return, a sense of having things back under more control.

Other people who self-harm say that the physical pain *distracts* them from the emotional pain temporarily, giving them a brief sense of peace and creating a diversion from their psychological distress.

Self-harm can mean many things to many people, but it is essentially a way to cope with internal emotional pain when that emotional pain is too great to endure. It can take any form, but common methods include cutting the skin, burning, scratching and pinching, as well as taking overdoses of medications or non-medical chemicals such as bleach. Some people punch hard surfaces to hurt themselves, and others pull out their hair.

It may be a regular coping strategy, something that some students do every time things feel overwhelming, or it may be a rare and occasional activity, to distract and survive the unbearable challenges that life throws at us. Some people self-harm just to feel "something, anything" because they feel so numb inside. Self-harming is *not* a "phase", "attention seeking", a "teenage thing", or "being melodramatic" (Knightsmith, 2018).

Why does self-harm matter?

It can be very hard for those who don't self-harm to understand why someone might take such action, but it is important for us all to try to remember just how bad someone will be feeling emotionally for them to want to physically harm themselves as a distraction.

Self-harm is actually an important "symptom" too of course, a sign that someone is suffering, possibly silently, and that they may be depressed or anxious, have an eating disorder, have a personality disorder, or be coping with other distressing issues.

Therefore, if you are someone who self-harms, it would be common for you to *also* be suffering from other mental health problems, so it is strongly recommended that you seek help from a kind and compassionate professional in order to explore what you are feeling, what may have led to the self-harm and any other difficulties you may be managing by yourself or with support from family and friends.

Self-harm may seem like it brings relief, so it may feel like it's a logical reaction if you are feeling dreadful. But unfortunately, it is also a *high-risk* activity, meaning that people who self-harm are also more at risk of suicide (Klonsky et al., 2013) or accidental death, so it is strongly recommended that you address the issues that are leading you to seek physical pain.

What help is available?

There is lots of help available for people who self-harm, both to support them with the underlying issues that have led to it and to help them when they feel like self-harming, or to distract them when they feel desperate. Some brilliant apps and websites exist and are listed in the Additional Resources section of this book, alongside phone and text support lines. And then, of course, there is actual psychological therapy (3–12 sessions are recommended by NICE, the UK's National Institute for Health and Care Excellence) which you can try, to help you move forward.

Speak to your doctor for a referral to a psychologist or specialist team for this psychological treatment.

Try this
When you are feeling like you might harm yourself, distract yourself by thinking of your favourite song lyrics and repeating them in your head.

An alternative is to call someone who loves you and who will be supportive even if they don't know how you're feeling right now. Have a chat with them – the urge to self-harm will pass and you can relax a little.

Suicidal thinking and behaviour

When life feels unbearable, pointless, futile or worthless, it is not uncommon to consider whether you really want to keep going, stay alive or bother with life. You might say things like "What's the point?", think you are a burden to others, and you may feel "trapped" in your life, aimless and unmotivated to carry on. All of these thoughts can lead you to consider taking your own life, and such suicidal thoughts can be very frightening and exhausting.

It may be helpful to know that up to 1 in 5 people will have suicidal thoughts at some point in their adult lives (De Leo et al., 2005), but for most people these are fleeting thoughts and are often just in response to overwhelming stress. They settle and pass, and we move on with our lives.

Some people are more likely to struggle with thoughts of suicide – for example students who have been bereaved by suicide themselves, or LGBTQ+ students, asylum seekers or refugees. Universities provide support for all these students and more, so talking to someone is the first step to getting help.

For most people who think about suicide, the negative feelings (feeling worthless, useless, unwanted or numb) will be temporary – and the person will go on to lead a life with normal ups and downs, no longer experiencing suicidal thoughts. It is important to remember that even such difficult thoughts can be tolerated and managed, then left behind, in time. The key is to talk to someone you trust.

Help for suicidal thinking

If suicidal thoughts are more persistent or plans start to form in your mind, or you prepare for taking your own life (such as by stockpiling tablets, writing a note, reading about methods online, or giving away your pet) then it is ***really important*** to seek help and talk to a professional such as a counselor, doctor or psychologist on the *same day*, especially if these thoughts are escalating or feel overpowering.

> **I Need Help NOW!**
> Immediate help is *always* available for suicidal thoughts.
>
> In the UK, dial 999, speak to your doctor, or go to the local hospital emergency department. Or call 111 and press option 2 for mental health support. Organizations like Samaritans are also available 24/7, by phone or text. (Tel 116 123 – free call.)
>
> In the US, call 988.
>
> Worldwide, go to findahelpline.com for help options.

Specialists and therapists *want* to hear from you. That is what they are there for, and so please do let them know if you are feeling like this.

Safety plans

Something that a lot of people are now doing and finding helpful is writing themselves a "safety plan" for use when times feel dark, or thoughts become very negative.

Safety plans are a tool (a set of instructions if you like) that you can turn to when suicidal thoughts feel overwhelming. You might have created one when you weren't feeling too bad, preferably with the support of a professional or even a university personal tutor.

The idea is to make a list (on paper, on your phone / laptop, or on specially designed apps) of activities to try when you feel yourself going down into a spiral of negativity. It can include useful resources, phone numbers and websites, as well as trusted people to contact and speak to if life feels overwhelmingly difficult at that moment. The plan should be kept somewhere you can easily find it when needed, and should start with noting the signs to look out for that indicate you are going downhill emotionally. List some activities that always make you feel a bit better (going for a walk, listening to a particular song, or watching a comedy programme) and then list the people to contact and emergency numbers if needed.

It can help to give yourself written instructions of how to keep yourself safe ("give housemate stockpiled medication") and also to include some positive reasons for living (your family, your pet, your love of music) and so on. You can share the plan with a trusted friend or family member if you like.

Finally, you should commit to trying to use the plan, though it is not a contract – it is just a commitment to yourself to read it and act on it when you are down.

Try this
Make your own safety plan now.

	Safety Plan
What makes you think about harming yourself (triggers)?	
Reasons for living	

	Safety Plan
Making things safe e.g., removal of access to means	
Activities that improve your mood	
Activities to calm yourself	
Contacts (general support)	

48 | SELF-HARM AND SUICIDAL THOUGHTS AND FEELINGS

	Safety Plan
Contacts (suicide and self-harm prevention-specific)	
Contacts (professional e.g., doctor / counseling service)	
Contacts (emergency)	
Personal commitment to implement safety plan	

CHAPTER 7

I THINK I HAVE DEPRESSION – WHAT DO I DO NEXT?

A lot of help is available at university and through your country's health system, though sometimes finding the right person to help you can be tricky.

It is common to hear students (and sometimes their parents) comment that someone at the university "should have known" that they were depressed or unwell, but it is important to remember that universities usually have tens of thousands of students to support, so there is more of an expectation that, as young adults, university students will reach out for support if they need it.

So, if you are unsure, then it is absolutely fine (and welcomed, in fact) to reach out and ask for advice or help, even if you think you might be wasting people's time. Nobody minds! They would much rather see students at an *early* stage of distress or concern than wait for things to become worse and potentially disastrous.

> **Talk to someone**
> The big message here is *please talk to someone* – a friend, family member, personal tutor, spiritual advisor, counselor, psychologist or a doctor.
> They are all there to support you and help.
> *Please talk to them!*

Friends and housemates supporting each other

It is well recognized that the first person many students will talk to about mental health or wellbeing worries is a friend or housemate. This is fine in general, as long as the friend is okay with it and not overwhelmed by the scale of your issues or their own problems. So, if the person you talk to seems keen to support you but also asks you to seek professional help, please listen to them and book an appointment. They may be feeling worried about you or have stuff going on that you don't know about, or they may have personal insight – for example, from an experience that you are unaware of (perhaps their mum had depression). They might then recognize the signs that require expert advice.

Either way, while it is fine to talk to friends first, they are not experts nor are they objective, and they also have their own lives to juggle. So do support each other, but please also talk to the professionals.

> **University professionals available for mental health support**
>
> - Wellbeing advisors
> - Counselors
> - Mental health advisors

- Disability teams
- Doctors and nurses
- Mental health nurses (Community Psychiatric Nurses)
- Psychologists
- Psychological wellbeing practitioners
- Psychiatrists

So why doesn't everyone with a mental health or psychological concern seek help? What is stopping many of the students who are suffering with anxiety, depression or other symptoms, from approaching any of these people or resources? Because sadly a significant number of people with mental health issues *do not* seek help.

Reasons you might not ask for help (Czyz et al., 2013)

- You don't think that you need help or you may not recognize that you have symptoms.
- You haven't got time to seek help, and it might interrupt your studies.
- You hope that you can sort it out yourself and don't feel you need professional help.
- You believe that others are more deserving or in need of support than you are, and you don't want to take up an appointment.
- You fear stigma or discrimination from others.
- You stigmatize yourself (i.e., you are harshly critical of yourself for having these issues) (Boerema et al., 2016).
- You don't think you have had the problems for very long, in your view.
- You worry that other people won't be supportive and understanding.

- You lack trust in professionals and worry about confidentiality.
- You worry that the professionals that you talk to will lack expertise in the topic (Berridge et al., 2017).
- You don't believe in biological (medical), or psychological-based explanations for mental health issues (Van Voorhees et al., 2006).
- You have previously experienced poor-quality support or treatment.

Let's explore these reasons in a little more detail, as these may be what is standing between you and a healthy, depression-free life!

You don't think that you need help, or you may not recognize that you have symptoms

One of the commonest questions that I'm asked by young people is: "How would I know if I have a mental health problem?" Essentially the answer is that if you don't feel well, you think something is wrong, or you are not getting the things done that you would expect or need to do (such as your work or meeting people and making friends) – or if you are worrying about any of this – then *talk to a professional* to check it out. You have nothing to lose, and that's what they are there for.

Wellbeing and healthcare professionals are trained to ask the right questions and put it all together. Then they'll share their opinion with you about whether or not the feelings you are having are in fact normal and to be expected, or whether you need additional support or even treatment.

If you don't feel right, then don't suffer in silence. Talk to someone. It is good to talk to friends and family of course, but that may not be quite enough if you are still feeling depressed. So, try to talk to someone who has experience in working with mental health problems.

And remember, talking to professionals is confidential.

You haven't got time to seek help and it might interrupt your studies
Maybe we should look at this another way: "You haven't got time to be unwell."

Life is busy, there's no doubt about that. But without your health and, in particular, your psychological health, then it's going to be tough to do all the amazing things you want to do, especially at university. So go on – take five minutes to go online, register with whichever service you want to talk to and book an appointment. It may be the best thing you do this year.

You believe that others are more deserving or in need of support than you are, and you don't want to take up an appointment
Following the pandemic, so many people have struggled with depression that it is understandable that some students could feel that they don't want to bother wellbeing teams. You may think that the professionals will be snowed under and that your case won't be as serious as someone else's, or that you should put yourself at the back of the queue. This is considerate but unnecessary, as you deserve support just as much as any other student, of course. But also, you may be struggling more than you realize, and only an objective wellbeing professional will be in a good place to advise on this. So go on, be kind to yourself and book that appointment!

You hope that you can sort it out yourself, and don't feel you need professional help
Well, it is certainly not unreasonable to try to help yourself before seeking professional help, of course, but if you have given it a month or so – using reliable, credible, professionally written resources (see the resources at end of

this book) – then it is probably time to run it past a trained counselor, psychologist or doctor.

There are loads of brilliant self-help options to try, from books to apps to online resources, and being able to say that you tried them first will also show how motivated and engaged you are, so that's a bonus. But everyone needs help sometimes. We are humans and are evolved to be social creatures, so give yourself a break and allow yourself to be supported by other (compassionate) humans.

You fear stigma or discrimination from others or you stigmatize yourself (i.e., you are harshly critical of yourself for having these issues)

Stigma and discrimination – if it's not other people, then we do it to ourselves. As if life wasn't tough enough, other people criticize us (or we fear that they will) for being human and having emotions, which sometimes get a little overwhelming. The only way to fight this one is to push past their (and sometimes our own) judgemental comments (real or imagined) and ask for help anyway. You are worth it.

Other people's opinions may be ill-informed and narrow minded, so you shouldn't value or listen to what they say anyway. You can do this!

You haven't had the problems for very long, in your view

If you've had the issues for more than a month, and especially if you've tried to help yourself along the way, then you really shouldn't wait any longer before talking to someone. Life is precious and you shouldn't spend it at the mercy of your mental health issues. There are fantastic and effective treatments out there, so don't spend any more time struggling, and the sooner you start a treatment the sooner it can have a positive effect. Also, you may have to join a waiting list for a bit, so best to get signed up and in the queue, if that's the case.

You worry that other people won't be supportive and understanding

It can be difficult to predict how people might react when you tell them you are struggling or need help, but sometimes they will be more understanding and supportive than you might expect. Even if they are less helpful, try not to let that stop you looking after yourself and getting the help you need.

Sometimes the people we care about most are unable to be as fully supportive as we might hope, but that is their issue, not ours. We can only take responsibility for our own lives.

You lack trust in professionals – you may be concerned about confidentiality

Health and wellbeing professionals all work to *strict standards of confidentiality*, and have their own professional guidance about keeping information confidential, which they follow carefully. No professional should share your information without discussing this option with you first, and in very limited circumstances they will consider sharing it if it is in your best interests.

In the rare cases when a professional needs to share your information without your agreement (consent), it would only be if you or someone else was considered to be in immediate (usually life-threatening) danger. They will do their best to seek your consent in these cases too. They cannot share information with future employers, and you will *always* be asked for your consent before medical information is requested or shared, and that includes for the Armed Forces.

For example, if a person develops a psychotic condition (they lose the ability to recognize that they are ill) and they are likely to hurt themselves or someone else, then a healthcare professional may have to disclose information. And, as mentioned, they will try to obtain consent *before* doing so.

The same would be true for suicidal thinking or if a person was considered to be at high risk of severe self-harm.

Students do worry about the sharing of their confidential information, but this is rarely done, and certainly not without consent. It is only done in circumstances where the student themselves will benefit and has given their consent, for example to plan better therapy or to ask for a second, expert opinion.

You worry that professionals that you talk to will lack specialist expertise in the topic

The people who choose to work with students, such as those in university support and health services, do so because they specifically enjoy working with young people and usually have additional training and expertise in the issues that most commonly affect young adults. For example, 50% of consultations in university health centres are for a mental health problem (Institute of Public Policy Research, 2017), and so the doctors working in these locations tend to have a great deal of experience in managing mental health issues.

They will often work closely with specialist doctors such as psychiatrists, and with psychologists. The university counselors and wellbeing practitioners are similarly highly trained, and stay up to date with both mandatory and voluntary training programmes and appraisal.

All of these professionals are familiar with the wide variety of mental health issues that affect young people, and have specialist skills to help them manage students' individual problems. In fact, university support services are probably the most expert teams in caring for student mental health issues.

You don't believe in biological or psychological-based explanations for mental health issues

Some people have a different understanding of emotional difficulties, perhaps believing it to be a spiritual issue,

CHAPTER 8

HELPFUL AND UNHELPFUL THINGS PEOPLE TRY TO ALLEVIATE THEIR DEPRESSION

There are, of course, many things that are well recognized to improve your mood, and it's important to try to give them a go if you can, as they may help you at a difficult time. Avoiding doing these things or engaging in behaviours such as drinking too much alcohol or taking drugs such as cannabis will undoubtedly make mood disorders worse, so it may be helpful to talk to a professional about your personal situation and what actions you can take to improve things.

Some of these suggestions may not have occurred to you before, or you may initially think, *"Uh-uh, no way!"* But keep an open mind, and let's see how we get on...

Exercise

We all know exercise is good for us and boosts our "happy hormones", and in fact research has shown that exercise can be enough to help some people make huge strides in overcoming depression (Mayo Clinic, 2023). But if you feel depressed, it can be near impossible to motivate yourself to get out there and do stuff. So be kind to yourself. Go for a walk, maybe in a part of town or the countryside that you haven't visited before.

As a student, it's easy to stick to the same old routes and areas that you know, but try branching out, go into the residential areas, the parks, the waterfronts and the great outdoors, and this will also neatly tick off another fantastic way to feel better…

> **Try this**
> Look at the tourist website for your university town or city and pick a recommended area to visit and walk around, maybe even join a walking tour for an hour or two. Then explore that new area on foot – it will distract you and get you outside and exercising, which is all helpful when you're feeling low.

Go outside

Being in nature is a really good way to feel better. Sometimes just experiencing "weather" (it doesn't have to be sunny) can blow you around a bit and make you feel something other than down or flat. It can take you away from your thoughts, distract you and pass the time. There is something restorative and refreshing about walking or running outside, by water, up a hill, under trees, or just lying on the grass, staring at the sky. It connects you with the world around you and shifts perspective. At an absolute minimum, it ensures you get your daily dose of vitamin D if you are outside for 20 minutes with some sun on your skin. Bonus!

Eat well (and minimize the alcohol!)

When you feel down, sometimes the easiest thing is just to stop eating, or eat crisps and junk food. It's minimum effort, provides a few calories and the body is kept alive… and while this exhausted and depressed way to sustain yourself is totally understandable, it probably isn't helping your mood, and it may actually be making things worse.

So, try to choose simple things to eat that still involve minimum effort while you're recovering, but are perhaps a little more helpful to your wellbeing.

Just as a reminder, alcohol is a depressant – in other words, it will actually make you feel more down and will make the quality of your sleep poorer, so the less you drink the better you will feel overall.

Get a plant (or a pet!)

Being a student means it can be really difficult to have something that you can nurture and care for in the privacy of your own room (like a dog), but a lot of students have told me how having a plant to look after, or even a pet goldfish, hamster or rat if allowed, has transformed their lives.

Humans are generally nurturing and enjoy looking after others, so caring for another being (whether animal or vegetable) can be uplifting and boost your happy hormones (like oxytocin). It's important to check the rules of wherever you are living, of course, and ensure that you have the time and energy to care for the plant or pet. But if you can, it might be the change that helps you turn the corner and lift your mood.

Try this
Buy a plant for your room – something robust and resilient (not an orchid, unless you're a particularly experienced gardener!) to care for day-to-day. Read up about what attention and watering it needs and really make an effort to look after it properly. You will feel a bit more connected to the world, and it will brighten up your room, bringing the outside in!

> **Bethany's story**
> Bethany was a second-year student and finding her course challenging. She was in a hectic, noisy, shared house with housemates and had a pretty strict (non-pet-friendly) landlord. At home she had had lots of pets and was used to the company of animals, but at university, she really missed her non-human support network. She chatted with a welfare professional at the university as she noticed her mood getting lower and her sleep becoming erratic. She told them about how she missed her pets, and so they suggested that she consider working as a local dogwalker, advertising to university staff and doing just enough to bring her comfort but not enough to interfere with her studies. Bethany was thrilled with the outcome, as her regular dog walks were helping out the staff who cared for her at university, and she benefited from the pets as therapy. Her mood lifted over the following weeks, and she continued more energized through her second year.

Help others

In the same way that nurturing a pet can help you feel better, helping others directly can also be beneficial. When you are very depressed it can feel almost impossible, but you might start just by "being in the room", for example literally being present at a charity cake / book sale, supporting a friend doing a 5km (3-mile) sponsored run and so on, and then you might feel like doing something yourself, for example, volunteering a couple of hours in a charity store.

guidelines are updated and protocols developed. Many universities now train their wellbeing and mental health teams in cultural competency to reduce the risk of racism, bias or a lack of cultural understanding, and recruit therapists and advisors from a much more diverse range of backgrounds. This increased sensitivity to the wide range of students' needs is one way in which support at university has improved dramatically over the last few years.

What you were offered before may not be what you are offered again. Moving to a new clinical specialist or therapist may be a step change for you, and lead to different, even brilliant, results.

It's got to be worth considering, hasn't it?

for example. Clearly, it is up to each individual to think about their wellbeing in terms that they are comfortable with, and it may be helpful to read about mental health on reliable and credible websites (see the resources at the back of this book), or in relevant books, if greater clarity and understanding are desired. But whatever your belief system for explaining mental health issues, there is help available to you.

Many universities have a chaplain, or religious or spiritual leader, for the campus community, who is often linked to local leaders of many faiths and backgrounds, so connecting with them might be a good first step in talking to someone empathic and compassionate about your depression. Chaplains, or other faith leaders, are happy to talk to students of all faiths, and those who follow none, and many students find it helpful to talk to someone caring and who understands campus life despite not being a healthcare or academic professional at the university. Whatever your beliefs, start the conversation and see if that helps to relieve some of your worries.

You have previously experienced poor-quality support or treatment

Everyone's experience of care is different, and can depend on a whole variety of factors such as waiting times, reception staff interaction, the attitudes and beliefs of the professional, or treatment side effects or results (benefits and failures). If you have had a previously poor experience, that is a real shame that it was negative. However, the good news is that trying something new or different, or even the same treatment with a different person, can have a different outcome.

Keep an open mind about the type of talking therapy offered, the nature of the therapist, the use of medication, or talking to friends and family about your experiences. Advances in medicine and therapy are made all the time;

Longer term, activities where you help others, for example helping children to learn to read, or collecting funds for third-sector organizations, can really give purpose to your life and make you feel good about yourself. And you meet new people!

Face time

No, not the screen version – real "human-to-human" face time. People have evolved to thrive when connecting with others, and we do best when we share experiences with other humans. It can be difficult, with rising loneliness and more of us spending time on our screens, to really meet people and connect with other humans, but if you can, meet up with a good, trusted friend and then just sit and chat (no phones). You will feel better for it, and it costs nothing.

It can be a real challenge to reach out when you feel down, so perhaps start with a message to let them know you are struggling and would appreciate their support. People love to help others (see previous point) so when they realize you aren't feeling great, a good friend will want to support you.

> **Try this**
> Just sitting with someone or going for a walk, side by side – not necessarily talking – can be therapeutic. If they are good at listening, and you feel able to talk, then that's a great combination. If you don't feel like talking yet, then just walk and experience being outside and getting some exercise.

Sleep rules!

Sleep must be one of *the* most underrated "activities" that humans can do to heal themselves! The importance of sleep as a process, and how we "miss it and mess with it" at our peril, needs to be emphasized.

There are some basic sleep rules to help us get the most out of this therapeutic pastime, so even if you do nothing else, trying to get your sleep back on track will be beneficial.

> **Try this**
> - Try to go to bed and get up at the same time every day, Monday to Sunday.
> - Try to be asleep when it's dark and awake when it's light, although within reason – for example between 10:30pm – 8:30am without sleeping in the daytime or staying up all night to work.
> - Stop all work and turn off all screens one hour before bedtime.
> - Spend that hour winding down, chatting with a friend, listening to quiet music, having a bath, reading quietly, or watching TV (nothing too scary or exciting!).
> - Exercise in the daytime before about 6pm, and don't have caffeine or alcohol late in the evening, nor eat any heavy meals.

Stick to these rules for about 4–6 weeks, and if that isn't working, check out CBT-I (which is CBT for Insomnia, an evidence-based technique to improve sleep). Make time to talk to a professional about how you are doing, as there may be other things that can help improve your sleep and mood.

Nic's story

Nic was a final-year student who came to the doctor as a last resort, as is often the case, unfortunately. He had become very low, numb and irritable with his housemates over the last few months and his girlfriend had "ordered" him to seek help. He wasn't sleeping and it was exhausting both of them. He would stay up late working, often until 3am, and then would try to sleep but be unable to relax. He would drink alcohol or smoke weed to try to lull himself into a sleepy state, but although it would work sometimes and get him off to sleep, he would then only sleep lightly and wake irritable and tetchy a few hours later. Being too exhausted at that point to get up, he would then sleep into the daylight hours and the cycle would begin again the next night.

Nic and the doctor had a long chat about the issues affecting him: his mood, his drinking, weed smoking and so on, and they pulled together a picture of his current mental state. They agreed that the first things to do were to reduce the alcohol intake, especially before bed, cut out the weed altogether, and then, over the next four weeks, adopt a strict sleep routine. The doctor explained all the "sleep rules" and gave him a leaflet about them. They agreed that they would meet again in four weeks and review Nic's progress.

Nic went away, and, with the support of his delighted girlfriend, he set about improving his daily habits. As the days passed and his new sleep routine settled down, he found himself being asleep when it was dark and up when it was light. His head felt clearer, his memory improved, and his brain fog lifted. His mood was still low, but he could now motivate himself to work in the daytime, and he started talking to a counselor. His full recovery took another few months, but tackling his sleep was the first step.

Avoid drugs

It is totally understandable that when life is garbage, you might want to block it out or take something to help you feel different or possibly better. When you take stuff you have found yourself, such as alcohol or drugs, it's called "self-medicating".

It doesn't usually work out well unfortunately, so if you are at this stage, then it's definitely time to talk to a counselor, psychologist or doctor about your worries. For example, long-term use of cannabis has been shown to reduce motivation, concentration and the ability to organize your thoughts, which the Royal College of Psychiatrists states "can cause particular problems for students" (2018).

CHAPTER 9

BEHAVIOUR BOOSTERS

If you think you have depression or are generally feeling low, you'll more than likely notice that you've stopped doing the things you used to enjoy. Where you used to exercise regularly, attend study groups or meet up with friends, you now find excuses to stay in your room in front of YouTube or Netflix. Even the thought of catching the bus to university or chatting to other students, including your housemates, makes you feel exhausted. Depression depletes energy and saps the enjoyment and sense of achievement you get from activities. In turn this starts a "vicious cycle" of not putting any effort into doing things or avoiding doing things, and therefore not getting anything back – no enjoyment or any sense of achievement!

To remedy this, you can use a **Behaviour Booster** – scheduling some activities into your week that you have previously enjoyed and / or from which you used to get a sense of purpose or achievement. Getting outside, exercising and talking to friends, etc., will help you feel better, and these are all examples of Behaviour Boosters. Behaviour Boosters have been shown to be an effective strategy in boosting mood and helping overcome depression (Dimidjian et al., 2006), and if you are waiting for CBT to start, it is likely that they will have you do this as the first step in treatment anyway!

Let's look at this idea in more detail using an example.

Behaviour Boosters in action

Jon used to attend a study group at the library. He enjoyed it for the social interaction and chance to chat to other students on his course, but also it gave him a sense of doing something productive. Recently Jon started feeling pretty down and low, and he was finding it really hard to motivate himself to go to classes and attend the study group. He forced himself to go to the study group last week, despite preferring to stay in his room and sleep. He found he didn't enjoy it as much as he used to, and although chatting to other students was okay, he didn't get as much of a buzz from it as before. Plus, he didn't feel like he learnt as much as other weeks – perhaps because he was finding it hard to pay attention. This week he is still feeling pretty low in his mood, so he has decided to skip the study group and just stay in his room instead.

Using a series of continuums, we can see that before Jon was depressed, he enjoyed the study group a lot (8/10 with 10 being the maximum enjoyment), it didn't feel like much effort to go along (3/10 with 10 being maximum effort), and he felt like he had achieved something (7/10 with 10 being maximum achievement).

Jon enjoyed study groups (8/10).

It took little effort to go to study group (3/10) – as in he was motivated to go, and it didn't feel very hard to get there.

And he got a sense of achievement after attending the study group (7/10).

Now let's look at the same scale when Jon began to feel down and when he last went to study group.

Jon got less enjoyment out of going to study group (3/10).

Jon found it much more of an effort to go to study group (8/10).

And he got a lower sense of achievement after going to study group (5/10).

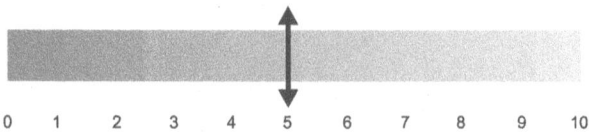

Now you'll see some of the scales are the opposite for Jon: he got little enjoyment from attending study group, felt as if he had achieved less as he normally did, and he had to make a much bigger effort to actually get to the library to attend the group.

You can see this is why people stop doing the things they enjoy as it takes so much more effort to get such little enjoyment or they feel less effective; it hardly seems worth it the effort!

So, if we examine the situation now, in the middle of depression, let's see what happens when Jon simply avoids going to the study group:

Jon gets no enjoyment out of study group.

It takes Jon no effort to avoid things.

> Jon also gets no sense of achievement from doing nothing.
>
>
>
>
>
> Jon is not getting *any* enjoyment or sense of achievement from study group! That seems a pretty bad outcome when you think about it. If Jon was able to make a big effort and attend this week, he might be able to extract that little bit of enjoyment out of going – 3/10 is still better than 0/10 for enjoyment! He might also find that it wasn't as bad as he had predicted, and that he maybe even got more than 3/10 along the enjoyment scale. Similarly, he will still feel a sense of achievement from going to study group, even if he found it hard to pay attention and didn't learn as much as he would usually when he is feeling better.

Using the scales from this example is an excellent way of showing yourself that, while you might only experience a small amount of enjoyment or get less of a sense of achievement from an activity compared to what you used to, it is better than having no enjoyment at all and feeling ineffectual. From this you can devise a diary in which you can plan a few activities ahead – nothing too heavy or too taxing, but small things that help you reconnect with the pleasures you once enjoyed, so they begin to feel effective again. It is also helpful to think about what you might need to do in order to achieve these things – such as telling a friend so they can check in with you after, or even join you for the activity. Setting these small, achievable goals is an excellent way of lifting your mood and feeling better.

To help, fill in the box on the next page. You should select activities that you used to enjoy, or ones that gave you a sense of being effective or achieving something.

The activities I would like to do this week are...
(e.g., go for a 10-minute jog, attend my psychology lecture)

I plan to do these activities on the following days at the following time
(e.g., Wednesday afternoon at 10am)

What things might help me to achieve these goals?
(e.g., asking my friend to join me, setting my alarm)

> **After the activity, describe how it went below. How much effort did it take? How much enjoyment did you get from it? Did you get a sense of achievement?**
>
> _____
> _____
> _____
> _____
> _____

> **Mark your rating from 1 to 10**
>
> Enjoyment ⃝   Effort ⃝   Achievement ⃝

If you are struggling with depression and feeling low, please try a Behaviour Booster. It seems like a simple idea, but it really works! Look at the study group example in this chapter and see how attending even if you don't feel like going is still more rewarding than staying at home. Behaviour Boosters really do work, and this is what a psychologist or therapist is likely to ask you do in the first place anyway. So, get ahead of the game and try it yourself first!

CHAPTER 10

TALKING THERAPIES

You have options

A variety of non-medication, evidence-based options are available for the treatment of depression. In other words, talking therapies work for depression in most cases.

This means that when you talk to a healthcare or counseling professional or psychologist about your symptoms and what your options are for getting better, you might discuss self-help (exercise, books, websites, etc.), mindfulness and individual and group therapies. Within the latter options, you might be offered CBT (Cognitive Behavioural Therapy), psychodynamic psychotherapy, interpersonal or other specialist therapeutic approaches (Health Improvement Scotland, 2010).

> **What is Cognitive Behavioural Therapy (CBT)?**
>
> We've mentioned CBT several times in this book already. So, let's take a closer look at what it is and how it can help. The aim of CBT is to change the way we respond or behave in response to what we are thinking and feeling.
>
> CBT is a really effective approach for depression. It looks at the links between the events in our lives, our interpretation of those events, and our responses to them.

Cognitions are the ways we think, what we believe, and how we interpret things. The way we *feel* is our emotional response to these things. And our *behaviours* are what we do in response to them, mentally or physically.

For example, *"I am a failure"* as a thought (cognition) can lead you to feel sad, numb and unable to do the things you want to do. This leads you to think you are even more of a "failure" (reinforcing the negative thoughts), and so it becomes a vicious cycle. This is sometimes called a "negative thought spiral".

CBT tries to break this cycle by training your mind to have a *new* reaction to negative thoughts and eventually to change the negative thoughts.

If we can change your thoughts, you can change your reactions and your behaviours. It may also work on tackling challenging situations you find yourself in, or alleviating physical symptoms in response to stress.

CBT is *not* a quick fix, and you may have to work hard by keeping a note of feelings, thoughts and actions between sessions. Your therapist will help you with this.

It focuses on the present, not the past.

Because everyone is different, and everyone's depression is different, there is no single solution, and it may take a couple of tries to find the right thing for you. CBT for depression can be delivered in many ways – self-help books, group or individual CBT session with a trained therapist, and these days there are online options and computerized CBT too, so don't be surprised if they are offered to you.

You may be able to self-refer to free local psychological therapy services – just search online for "free psychological therapy near me". Your university will also offer a variety of therapy options, and you may also consider trying online private therapy, or being connected to a therapist via an app.

The therapist

The therapist as a person and their personality, approach and field of expertise are also clearly important factors, so don't rush in and feel you have to commit to therapy with someone if you're not comfortable with them or confident with their knowledge.

Check they are working with an organization you trust or that they are registered with a nationally recognized professional membership organization. Speak to them or meet them at least once before committing to a series of sessions with them.

Waiting lists

There can sometimes be a wait for in-person therapy, so it may be that in the meantime you try online support with resources provided by your university – ask about free "bridging" support to get you through the waiting period. There may be drop-in sessions just to have someone to chat to when you need it.

Approaching your doctor is always an option if you're feeling bad and in need of support, and of course all universities have a variety of pastoral support, so check their website ("student support") for mental health advisors, wellbeing advisors, pastoral tutors and accommodation / residential staff who can help you while you wait for treatment.

Remember

The thing to remember here is that for *mild through to severe* depression, talking therapies are recommended – sometimes alongside medication – so it is really important to know that you *can* get better, even if it takes a bit of time to see the improvement with treatment. Don't give up – talking therapies can be hard work, but are really effective and definitely worth trying.

CHAPTER 11

WHEN MEDICATION IS THE NEXT STEP

These are some of the things that people say when discussing taking medication for depression, as reasons not to take them:

But here's something to think about...

You rarely hear people say those things about Type 1 diabetes, asthma or cancer.

People are very much more worried about being judged for taking medication for mental health problems than they are for physical health problems, which can make it really challenging for those who are keen to try something and are open minded about options. They might then feel criticized for not "beating" an illness without medical assistance, despite the fact we would not expect people to "beat" Type 1 diabetes without insulin.

Depression is a complex mental health illness which has shown clear and repeated benefit from medication over many years of scientific trials, and sufferers should feel able to try tablets if they are advised to do so by a qualified professional and if it feels appropriate in their individual situation.

Antidepressants are recommended for moderate to severe depression, but not mild depression. In fact, studies have repeatedly shown that antidepressant medication was *more effective* than placebo for moderate to severe depression (Kishi et al., 2022). In other words, the pills do work, but it's really important to find the *right* one for you – with the fewest side effects – if you are going to take them. Even if one type doesn't work, another might be great for you.

The advice here is to talk to a doctor, perhaps one with an interest in mental health or young people's health, and discuss your symptoms. You can then discuss whether medication might be an option for you. For many people it is unnecessary, but for others it can be transformational and literally life changing.

Some people need medication to sleep, function, balance their mood and be well enough to try talking therapies. For others it lifts them out of suicidal thoughts and reduces the need to self-harm.

Try to remain open minded about antidepressants and other medications for mental health conditions. As most of them will show whether or not they are working and are right for you within four weeks, and as side effects for most will also settle in that time (best to start with low or half doses for a week or so, to minimize side effects – ask your doctor), you can quite quickly see if you want to carry on with them or not, or change to a different brand and so on.

> **Try this**
> When you are waiting for treatment to start working (or to start at all) it may help to take one day at a time, doing small activities that nurture your soul. Try doing something like making a "duvet nest" on the sofa and watching your favourite comedy series or films, and / or baking fairy cakes or cookies (using a cake mix and ready-made icing if necessary), to feel productive and treat yourself to something tasty. Drawing or colouring in can also feel peaceful when you are very low and have no energy for more organized or demanding activities. Just one day at a time, sometimes one hour at a time, is all you need to focus on.

Starting, stopping and safe approaches

Certainly 6–8 weeks will be enough to give any medication a good "go", and if you don't like them, and if it's only been eight weeks or less, you can stop them gradually over 1–2 weeks. If you've been on them longer, the weaning period will be proportionately longer too (6–8 months of treatment, for example, will need 6–8 weeks weaning off to avoid withdrawal side effects).

Tell your doctor that you plan to stop and the reasons for it if you decide to do so independently, so that they can note it for future record. It may be helpful to discuss it with your doctor before stopping. Then if you do decide to try them again in future, they will know if a particular brand didn't suit you the last time and to try something different.

Common myths and misunderstandings about antidepressants

They're addictive

Modern antidepressants are not addictive. People worry about this a lot, but if you take them, you will need them for a period of time, just like you would antibiotics for an infection, then you will stop after a recommended medication course length.

In general, first-time treatment courses are for six months minimum, and if you need antidepressants for a relapse in future the course length is usually two years minimum. Some people do need longer courses than this, but most don't. You don't get addicted to them in that time, but you may need to stop them gradually to avoid withdrawal side effects.

Withdrawal (discontinuation) effects can include stomach upsets, electric shock sensations, anxiety, flu-like symptoms and headaches. They are common, but can be minimized by reducing your dose very slowly over a reasonable period of time. So taper the dose and wean off gradually!

Don't stop antidepressants suddenly if you've been taking them for more than 6–8 weeks. Talk to your doctor first if you are keen to stop.

Side effects will be dreadful

All medications can cause side effects. This is one thing that students ask about a lot, of course, but they sometimes forget that even headache tablets can have side effects for some people. So yes, side effects can be common, but are usually mild and settle quite quickly, especially if you start by taking *half* of the recommended treatment dose for at least a week. Discuss this with your doctor before starting.

Side effects can include jitteriness, headaches, sleep disturbance, anxiety, nausea, diarrhea and problems with having or enjoying sex (sexual dysfunction), so do ask about the particular medication you are being prescribed and what the issues might be.

Most side effects wear off after a week or two, but not all, so if they are intolerable it is important to go back to your doctor and discuss this. Different types of antidepressants have differing side effects too, so a switch to an alternative type may be all that's needed.

And they don't "change" who you are as a person or your personality; they help you to get back to normal and feel like yourself again.

If the first one doesn't work, none will

Many students have to try more than one type of antidepressant before finding the right one for them. But when they do, it can really transform their lives and they are so pleased that they persevered to find the one that suited them and works best.

I'm feeling better – I think I'll stop now

A common issue is that as the medication starts to work after a few weeks, people feel themselves return to normal and are keen to stop taking it. And so they do, believing themselves to be "cured" and the problem sorted. Unfortunately, the evidence is that antidepressants need to be taken for several (between 6 and 12) months after feeling better to have a sustained long-term benefit, so stopping them too early will likely lead to you relapsing and needing to take them again, or even feeling worse overall.

It's so important to embrace the improvements but not to stop taking the medication too soon. Just keep going, live your life, get on with your studies and activities, and keep checking in with your doctor, then plan to come off them when you have been feeling well and "normal" for at least six months (Royal College of Psychiatrists, 2020).

People who have a second episode of depression in their life will need to take them for two years after feeling better, and if you have a third episode you may need to take them for a few years. But everyone is different, so it's best to chat through with your own doctor of course.

Actually, the drugs do work!

In summary, medication is not for everyone or for every type of depression, but it does work in many cases and should definitely be considered on an individual basis after you've discussed your options carefully with a professional and considered the side effects and withdrawal planning for when you're ready to stop.

FINAL WORDS

Let's recap some of the key points about depression in case you are struggling or know someone who is.

Depression is truly awful, and when you're "in it", it can be hard to see a way out. But it does *not* have to be awful like this in the future. You *can* get better.

It takes time, and you may need to try different types of talking therapy or medication before you get there, but depression is a treatable illness. You just need to find the treatment that works for you and stick with it.

So many students say they wish they had asked for help sooner when they realize that their symptoms and feelings can be sorted out, addressed, and treated with the right professional help. Don't delay! Please talk to a professional soon.

Facts about depression

- Up to 1 in 3 people will suffer from depression at some point in their lives. This is higher than pre-pandemic levels.
- More women than men are affected.
- Nearly *half* of those diagnosed with depression *also* have an anxiety disorder.
- Eating disorders and depression frequently occur *together*.
- Up to 1 in 3 of people with a long-term health condition such as diabetes or arthritis will *also* have depression.

- You can have depression without feeling depressed; you might feel angry or numb, but not sad or low.
- People identifying as LGBTQ+ are more likely to suffer from depression.
- Women from BAME populations are more likely to suffer from depression than their non-BAME female peers.

Getting help

- Try the resources at the back of this book to learn more about depression, or to hear from people who have experienced it and can share their thoughts on how best to manage it.
- Talk to family or friends for everyday support.
- There are lots of self-help options for depression: exercise, being in nature, nurturing a pet or plant, connecting with others and helping them too, as well as mindfulness techniques, so start with these to see if you can take steps for yourself. You'll feel good for trying, and there's always more help if you are struggling.
- Try a Behaviour Booster for as a first step. It is an easy way to feel better and is very effective.
- Your university will provide some free help, for example in the form of counseling or wellbeing services.
- Many universities offer free online support too, so that's another option to consider if you aren't keen to talk face-to-face yet.
- Some local talking therapies are provided free.

Treatment options

- Lots of help is available, through talking therapies or medication.
- The main thing is to take the first step and talk to a professional about your options.
- No one will make you do anything you don't want to do.

- Services are confidential, so you can speak freely and share your worries.
- Therapy such as CBT (Cognitive Behavioural Therapy) will almost always be the first treatment you are offered if it's available.
- You may be offered group sessions, which can be a good first step for depression, if the waiting list for one-to-one support is long.
- If you try the talking therapy and it is not working even after a recommended amount of time, or your symptoms are severe and disabling, you may be offered medication to help you engage more fully with the talking therapy.
- Medication can work very well and effectively treat depression. There are many different types to try.
- You may need to take medication for several months. It is important not to stop it suddenly if you have been on it for longer than 6–8 weeks.
- A doctor should always be happy to discuss your personal situation and come to a decision with you about which medicine may be worth trying, as well as discussing potential side effects, how long to take it for, and any other concerns you may have.
- If the first type of medication you try does not work well for you, don't give up; chat with your doctor and consider other options.
- They should then contact you regularly to check all is going well.

ADDITIONAL RESOURCES

Depression

Websites

- NHS support **www.nhs.uk**
- The Mix **www.themix.org.uk**
- Mind **www.mind.org.uk** or call **0300 123 3393**
- Students Against Depression **www.studentsagainstdepression.org**
- Mental Health America **www.mhanational.org**
- Anxiety and Depression Association of America **adaa.org**
- Moodgym (for CBT skills) **www.moodgym.anu.edu.au**
- Beating the Blues (online treatment and support) **www.beatingtheblues.co.uk**
- Royal College of Psychiatrists **www.rcpsych.ac.uk**
- Student Minds (the UK national student mental health charity) **www.studentminds.org.uk**
- For sleep CBT-I **www.sleepstation.org.uk**

TEDx Talks

- "Why Big Boys Don't Cry" by Gareth Griffith
- "What I Learnt from 78,000 GP Consultations with University Students" by Dominique Thompson

Social media

- Dr Julie Smith **www.tiktok.com/@drjuliesmith**

Books

- *Reasons to Stay Alive* by Matt Haig
- *Sane New World* by Ruby Wax
- *The Stranger on the Bridge* by Jonny Benjamin
- *Overcoming Depression* by Paul Gilbert
- *Thrive* by Richard Layard and David M Clark (about the power of CBT)
- *The Upward Spiral* by Alex Korb

Self-harm and suicidal thinking

Websites

- In the UK: Samaritans **www.samaritans.org** or call **116 123** for free
- In the US: 988 Lifeline **988lifeline.org**
- The American Foundation for Suicide Prevention **afsp.org**
- Connecting with People **www.connectingwithpeople.org**
- Papyrus **www.papyrus-uk.org**
- Self-injury Support **www.selfinjurysupport.org.uk**
- Crisis Text Line USA **www.crisistextline.org**
- Self-harm UK **www.selfharm.co.uk**
- LifeSigns **www.lifesigns.org.uk**
- Harmless **www.harmless.org.uk**

Apps (all free)

- *distrACT* – an app for young people created by experts
- *Calm Harm* – www.calmharm.co.uk
- *My Coping Plan* – for writing your own safety plan
- *Student Health App* – for all health issues including mental health

REFERENCES

Alcohol & Drug Foundation. (2018). Drug Facts - Cannabis, Weed, Marijuana. Available at: https://adf.org.au/drug-facts/cannabis/

Anxiety & Depression Association of America. Depression. Available at: https://adaa.org/understanding-anxiety/depression

Benros, M., Waltoft, B., Nordentoft, M., et al. (2013). Autoimmune Diseases and Severe Infections as Risk Factors for Mood Disorders. Available at: https://jamanetwork.com/journals/jamapsychiatry/fullarticle/1696348

Berridge, B., McCann, T., Cheetham, A. & Lubman, D. (2018). Perceived Barriers and Enablers of Help-Seeking for Substance Use Problems During Adolescence. *Health Promotion Practice*. 19(1), 86–93.

Bignall, T., Jeraj, S., Helsby, E. & Butt, J. (2019). Racial disparities in mental health: Literature and evidence review. Available at: https://raceequalityfoundation.org.uk/wp-content/uploads/2022/10/mental-health-report-v5-2.pdf

Bipolar UK. (2018). I think I might have bipolar. Available at: www.bipolaruk.org/Pages/FAQs/Category/i-think-i-might-have-bipolar

Cipriani, A., Furukawa, T., Salanti, G., Chaimani, A., Atkinson, L., Ogawa, Y., Leucht, S., Ruhe, H., Turner, E, Higgins, J, Egger, M, Takeshima, N, Hayasaka, Y, Imai, H, Shinohara, K, Tajika, A, Ioannidis, J. & Geddes, J. (2018). Comparative efficacy and acceptability of 21 antidepressant drugs for the acute treatment of adults with major depressive disorder: a systematic review and network meta-analysis. *The Lancet*. 391(10128), 1357–66.

Curran, T. & Hill, A. (2017). Perfectionism is increasing over time: A meta-analysis of birth cohort differences from 1989 to 2016. *Psychological Bulletin*.

Czyz, E., Horwitz, A., Eisenberg, D., Kramer, A. & King, C. (2013). Self-reported Barriers to Professional Help Seeking Among College Students at Elevated Risk for Suicide. *Journal of American College Health*. 61(7), 398–406.

The Depression and Bipolar Support Alliance. (2014). Understanding Agitation. Available at: www.dbsalliance.org/pdfs/brochures/agitation.pdf

De Leo, D., Cerin, E., Spathonis, K. & Burgis, S. (2005). Lifetime risk of suicide ideation and attempts in an Australian community: Prevalence, suicidal process, and help-seeking behaviour. *Journal of Affective Disorders*. 86(2-3), 215–24.

Dimidjian, S., Hollon, S.D., Dobson, K.S., Schmaling, K.B., Kohlenberg, R.J., Addis, M.E. & Atkins, D.C. (2006). Randomized trial of behavioral activation, cognitive therapy, and antidepressant medication in the acute treatment of adults with major depression. *Journal of Consulting and Clinical Psychology*. 74(4), 658.

Gallup. (2023). U.S. Depression Rates Reach New Highs. Available at: https://news.gallup.com/poll/505745/depression-rates-reach-new-highs.aspx#:~:text=Those%20aged%20 18%20to%2029,depression%20or%20treatment%20for%20 depression

General Medical Council. (2015). Supporting medical students with mental health conditions. Available at: www.gmc-uk.org/education/standards-guidance-and-curricula/guidance/supporting-medical-students-with-mental-health-conditions

Health Improvement Scotland. (2010). Non-Pharmaceutical Management of Depression in Adults. Available at: www.sign.ac.uk/assets/sign114.pdf

Hewlett, K. (2001). Can low self-esteem and self-blame on the job make you sick? Available at: www.apa.org/monitor/julaug01/jobsick.aspx

Institute of Public Policy Research. (2017). Not by Degrees. Available at: www.ippr.org/files/2017-09/1504645674_not-by- degrees-170905.pdf

Kishi, T., Ikuta, T., Sakuma, K., et al. (2023). Antidepressants for the treatment of adults with major depressive disorder in the maintenance phase: a systematic review and network meta-analysis. *Mol Psychiatry*. 28, 402–409.

Klonsky, E., May, A. & Glenn, C. (2013) The relationship between nonsuicidal self-injury and attempted suicide: Converging evidence from four samples. *Journal of Abnormal Psychology*. 122(1), 231–37.

Knightsmith, P. (2018). In Our Hands. Available at: www.inourhands.com/skills-building/what-not-to-say-if-your-child-is-self-harming/

Lee, J., Lee, M., Liao, S., Chang, C., Sung, S., Chiang, H. & Tai, C. (2010). Prevalence of Suicidal Ideation and Associated Risk Factors in the General Population. *Journal of the Formosan Medical Association*. 109(2), 138–47.

Levinson, D. & Nichols, W. (2023). Major Depression and Genetics. Stanford Medicine. Available at: https://med.stanford.edu/depressiongenetics/mddandgenes.html#:~:text=Heritability%20is%20probably%20 40-50,(psychological%20or%20physical%20factors

Liu, W., Ge, T., Leng, Y., Pan, Z., Fan, J., Yang, W. & Cui, R. (2017). The Role of Neural Plasticity in Depression: From Hippocampus to Prefrontal Cortex. *Neural Plasticity*. 1–11.

Mayo Clinic. (2023). Depression and anxiety: Exercise eases symptoms. Available at: https://www.mayoclinic.org/

diseases-conditions/depression/in-depth/depression-and-exercise/art-20046495#:~:text=Regular%20exercise%20may%20improve%20depression,them%20over%20the%20long%20term

MedlinePlus. (2012). Tips for Getting A Good Night's Sleep. *NIH MedlinePlus the Magazine.* Available at: https://medlineplus.gov/magazine/issues/summer15/articles/summer15pg22.html

Mental Health America. (2018). Co-Occurring Disorders And Depression. Available at: www.mentalhealthamerica.net/conditions/co-occurring-disorders-and-depression

Mental Health Foundation. (2018). Mental health statistics: black, Asian and minority ethnic groups. Available at: www.mentalhealth.org.uk/statistics/mental-health-statistics-black-asian-and-minority-ethnic-groups

Mental Health Foundation. (2018). Mental health statistics: LGBT people. Available at: www.mentalhealth.org.uk/statistics/mental-health-statistics-lgbt-people

Mind. Facts and figures about racism and mental health. Available at: https://www.mind.org.uk/about-us/our-strategy/becoming-a-truly-anti-racist-organisation/facts-and-figures-about-racism-and-mental-health/

Naylor, C. (2012). Long term conditions and mental health. The King' Available at: www.kingsfund.org.uk/sites/default/files/field/field_publication_file/long-term-conditions-mental-health-cost-comorbidities-naylor-feb12.pdf

NHS. (2022). Seasonal affective disorder (SAD). Available at: www.nhs.uk/conditions/seasonal-affective-disorder-sad/

NHS Digital. (2016). Adult Psychiatric Morbidity Survey: Survey of Mental Health and Wellbeing, England, 2014. Available at: https://digital.nhs.uk/data-and-information/publications/statistical/adult-psychiatric-morbidity-survey/adult-psychiatric-morbidity-survey-survey-of-mental-health-and-wellbeing-england-2014

Nie, X., Kitaoka, S., Tanaka, K., Segi-Nishida, E., Imoto, Y., Ogawa, A., Nakano, F., Tomohiro, A., Nakayama, K., Taniguchi, M., Mimori-Kiyosue, Y., Kakizuka, A., Narumiya, S. & Furuyashiki, T. (2018). The Innate Immune Receptors TLR2/4 Mediate Repeated Social Defeat Stress-Induced Social Avoidance through Prefrontal Microglial Activation. *Neuron*. 99(3), 464–79.

NICE. (2013). Self-harm. Available at: https://pathways.nice.org.uk/pathways/self-harm#path=view%3A/pathways/self-harm/longer-term-management-of-self-harm-assessment-and-treatment.xml&content=view-node%3Anodes-interventions-for-self-harm

Owens, M., Townsend, E., Hall, E., Bhatia, T., Fitzgibbon, R. & Miller-Lakin, F. (2022). Mental Health and Wellbeing in Young People in the UK during Lockdown (COVID-19). *Int J Environ Res Public Health*. 19(3), 1132.

Pan American Health Organization. (2019). Mental health problems are the leading cause of disability worldwide, say experts at PAHO Directing Council side event. Available at: https://www3.paho.org/hq/index.php?option=com_content&view=article&id=15481:mental-health-problems-are-the-leading-cause-of-disability-worldwide-say-experts-at-paho-directing-council-side-event&Itemid=0&lang=en#gsc.tab=0

Raison, C., Capuron, L. & Miller, A. (2006). Cytokines sing the blues: inflammation and the pathogenesis of depression. *Trends in Immunology*. 27(1), 24–31.

Rakesh, D. (2018). The immune system and the pathogenesis of depression. Medium. Available at: https://medium.com/lazy-synapse/the-immune-system-and-the-pathogenesis-of-depression-8b0ab5725965

Royal College of Psychiatrists. (2018). Cannabis and mental health. Available at: www.rcpsych.ac.uk/mentalhealthinfo/problems/alcoholanddrugs/cannabisandmentalhealth.aspx

Royal College of Psychiatrists. (2020). Antidepressants. Available at: https://www.rcpsych.ac.uk/mental-health/treatments-and-wellbeing/antidepressants

Serico, C. (2015). 'Have faith': See Dwayne Johnson's inspiring advice for people with depression. *Today*. Available at: www.today.com/health/dwayne-rock-johnson-shares-inspiring-message-people-depression-t56586

Statista. (2021). Share of young people who reported experiences of depression/feeling down in the United Kingdom (UK) from 2009 to 2021. Available at: https://www.statista.com/statistics/1199302/depression-among-young-people-in-the-united-kingdom/

Student Health Doc Blog. (2013). A student's account of depression. Available at: https://studenthealth.blogs.bristol.ac.uk/2013/06/20/a-students-account-of-depression/

University of Manchester. (2018). Centre for Mental Health and Safety. Available at: http://research.bmh.manchester.ac.uk/cmhs

Van Voorhees, B., Fogel, J., Houston, T., Cooper, L., Wang, N. & Ford, D. (2006). Attitudes and illness factors associated with low perceived need for depression treatment among young adults. Social Psychiatry and Psychiatric Epidemiology. 41(9), 746–54.

Weitzman, M., Rosenthal, D. & Liu, Y. (2011). Paternal Depressive Symptoms and Child Behavioral or Emotional Problems in the United States. *PEDIATRICS*. 128(6), 1126–34.

World Health Organization. (2018). Depression. Available at: www.who.int/en/news-room/fact-sheets/detail/depression

World Health Organization. (2018). Mental disorders. Available at: www.who.int/news-room/fact-sheets/detail/mental-disorders

TriggerHub is one of the most elite and scientifically proven forms of mental health intervention

Trigger Publishing is the leading independent mental health and wellbeing publisher in the UK and US. Our collection of bibliotherapeutic books and the power of lived experience changes lives forever. Our courageous authors' lived experiences and the power of their stories are scientifically endorsed by independent federal, state and privately funded research in the US. These stories are intrinsic elements in reducing stigma, making those with poor mental health feel less alone, giving them the privacy they need to heal, ensuring they are guided by the essential steps to kick-start their own journeys to recovery, and providing hope and inspiration when they need it most.

Clinical and scientific research conducted by assistant professor Dr Kristin Kosyluk and her highly acclaimed team in the Department of Mental Health Law & Policy at the University of South Florida (USF), as well as complementary research by her peers across the US, has independently verified the power of lived experience as a core component in achieving mental health prosperity. Their findings categorically confirm lived experience as a leading method in treating those struggling with poor mental health by significantly reducing stigma and the time it takes for them to seek help, self-help or signposting if they are struggling.

Delivered through TriggerHub, our unique online portal and smartphone app, we make our library of bibliotherapeutic titles and other vital resources accessible to individuals and organizations anywhere, at any time and with complete privacy, a crucial element of recovery. As such, TriggerHub is the primary recommendation across the UK and US for the delivery of lived experiences.

At Trigger Publishing and TriggerHub, we proudly lead the way in making the unseen become seen. We are dedicated to humanizing mental health, breaking stigma and challenging outdated societal values to create real action and impact. Find out more about our world-leading work with lived experience and bibliotherapy via triggerhub.com, or by joining us on:

- @triggerhub_
- @triggerhub.org
- @triggerhub_

Dr Kristin Kosyluk, PhD, is an assistant professor in the Department of Mental Health Law and Policy at USF, a faculty affiliate of the Louis de la Parte Florida Mental Health Institute, and director of the STigma Action Research (STAR) Lab. Find out more about Dr Kristin Kosyluk, her team and their work by visiting:

USF Department of Mental Health Law & Policy:
www.usf.edu/cbcs/mhlp/index.aspx

USF College of Behavioral and Community Sciences:
www.usf.edu/cbcs/index.aspx

STAR Lab: www.usf.edu/cbcs/mhlp/centers/star-lab/

For more information, visit **BJ-Super7.com**

www.ingramcontent.com/pod-product-compliance
Ingram Content Group UK Ltd.
Pitfield, Milton Keynes, MK11 3LW, UK
UKHW041056160925
2946IPUK00015B/79